THE 10 LARGEST NATIVE AMERICAN TRIBES

US HISTORY 3RD GRADE

Children's American History

BABY PROFESSOR
EDUCATION KIDS

Speedy Publishing LLC
40 E. Main St. #1156
Newark, DE 19711
www.speedypublishing.com

In this book, we're going to talk about the 10 largest Native American tribes. So, let's get right to it!

Native American dancers at the NYC Pow Wow in Brooklyn.

Native Americans were living in North and South America before Christopher Columbus arrived in 1492. He called the natives "Indians" because he mistakenly thought that he had arrived in India. He didn't realize that he was in a different region of the world and India was thousands of miles away.

Group of Native Americans in traditional outfits.

No one knows exactly how many Native Americans lived in North and South America when the New World was "discovered." Historians don't have enough information to accurately estimate the population numbers since there was no official census at that time. Some scholars believe the estimate to be about

Illustration of Sioux encampment.

10 million people and others say around 50 million. The arrival of white settlers caused disastrous consequences for the Native Americans. Their way of life was destroyed as the European settlers took over the land that was once theirs.

WHEN DID THE NATIVE AMERICAN PEOPLE ARRIVE IN THE AMERICAS?

There is still debate among archaeologists as to which groups of people first migrated to the Americas. For a long time, it was believed that prehistoric races of hunters came to the Americas from the northeastern regions of Asia. At the time they traveled, about 12,000 years ago, there was an Ice Age and there was a bridge of land from Siberia to Alaska.

Old illustration of a Tepee in Comanche Native American camp.

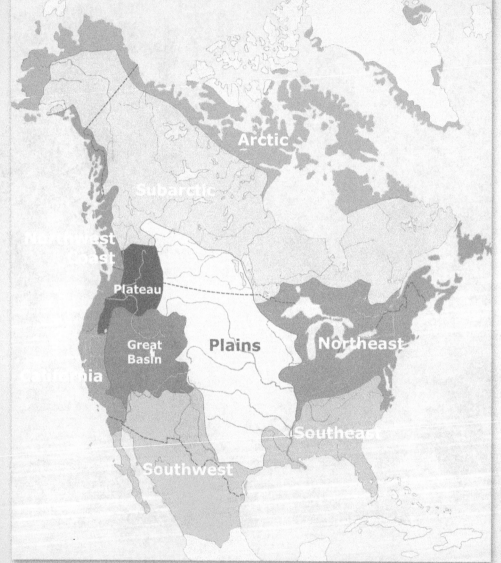

Arctic

Subarctic

Northwest Coast

Plateau

Great Basin

Plains

Northeast

California

Southeast

Southwest

Many Native Americans have similar physical features to people who originally lived in Mongolia as well as those populations who lived in China and Siberia. It also makes sense that these hardy people who knew how to survive in the extreme cold of places like Siberia would still be able to thrive in the cold environment of Alaska.

The Cultural areas of pre-Columbian North America.

In the 1930s, remains of mammoths were found near Clovis, New Mexico. With these remains were some stone arrowheads. When these artifacts were dated, they were proven to be about 11,500 years old. Archaeologists believed that this site was the first proof of the date of human habitation in the Americas.

American bird point arrowhead and spearhead found in Kentucky made around 2000 to 6000 years ago.

Beautiful young Mongolian lady in the late afternoon sun.

Over the last twenty years, there have been some surprising discoveries that challenge what archaeologists thought before. In 1996, at a dig in Chile, weapons as well as tools that dated back 12,500 years were found. In Brazil, a woman's skeleton was found that dates back

A group of Aboriginal kids washing themselves in a river.

at least 11,000 years. The surprising thing about this skeleton was that her facial features didn't match with the Mongolian peoples. Instead, they more closely resemble Australian's Aboriginal people. The Aboriginal people date back 60,000 years and came from the first humans in Africa.

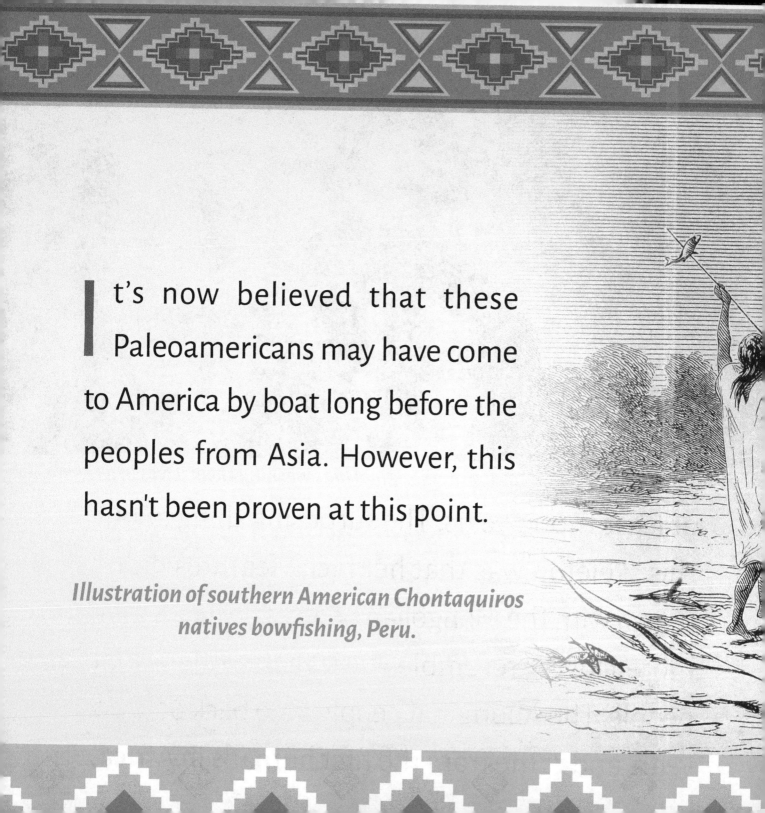

It's now believed that these Paleoamericans may have come to America by boat long before the peoples from Asia. However, this hasn't been proven at this point.

Illustration of southern American Chontaquiros natives bowfishing, Peru.

One thing is clear. No matter who the first people in the Americas were, they were the ancestors of the Native Americans. They had dominion over the land for a full 11,000-12,000 years before the Europeans grabbed up their lands for their expansion plans.

Old illustration of Sioux woman carrying child on her shoulder.

HOW MANY TRIBES WERE THERE WHEN THE EUROPEANS ARRIVED?

It's difficult to say how many distinct tribes of Native Americans there were when European settlers first arrived. Today, in the United States alone, there are 562 Indian Nations. About 229 of these Nations are located in the state of Alaska.

The San Manuel Band of Indians annual Pow Wow in San Bernardino.

The remaining Indian Nations are located in 33 other states. Some historians estimate that there were as many as 1,000 tribes or more in the land that is now the United States when European settlers first arrived.

Illsutration of Mohave people, Native American.

WHAT HAPPENED WHEN THE EUROPEANS ARRIVED

Europeans began coming to the New World right away and over time millions of immigrants made the New World their home. As the settlers from Europe, Asia, and Africa increased, the Native Americans began to decrease in numbers. Some of the decrease was through warfare, but many Native Americans died from the diseases the settlers brought with them, such as bubonic and pneumonic plagues, influenza, and small pox.

White man prisoner in a Native American tepee.

The Native Americans had no immunity to these diseases, so once they contracted them, there was slim chance they would survive.

WHAT IS A TRIBE?

When scholars study populations of Native Americans and their history, they are often organized into tribes or nations. Members of the same tribe would have shared many common characteristics. They would have had the same language, or if they spoke dialects, those dialects would be related. They would have shared religious beliefs. They would also have had the same customs and culture.

Native American dwelling known as a hogan.

Another way of studying the different tribes is to understand where they were living and what types of environments they had adapted to. In the United States, Canada, and Mexico there were seven different major regions and within those regions there were numerous tribes.

Geronimo (1829-1909), Chiricahua Apache warrior in Indian clothing and feathered headdress, 1907.

Native Indian women dance during annual Squamish Nation Pow Wow.

REGIONS WHERE THE NATIVE AMERICANS LIVED

The ancestors of the Native Americans in North America lived as far north as the Arctic and as far south as Mexico.

ARCTIC AND SUBARCTIC REGIONS

This region has incredibly cold temperatures- some of the coldest on planet Earth. One notable group that lived in this region is the **Inuit People.** This Alaskan tribe ate a diet of meat from whales and seals.

Smiling Eskimo woman wearing traditional clothing

NORTHWEST COAST AND PLATEAU REGIONS

This region of the United States and Canada is heavily forested. The Native Americans there used cedar planks to construct their houses and they built elaborate totem poles to tell important stories. The **Nez Perce** tribe, the **Salish** tribe, and the **Tlingit** tribe lived in these regions.

The Totem Pole carvings representing indigenous and first nation people.

CALIFORNIAN REGION

The **Mohave** tribe and the **Miwok** tribe lived on the land that is now the state of California.

GREAT BASIN REGION

Because this area of the United States is very dry, the Europeans were not settling it in large numbers so the tribes there were left alone for a while. Notable Great Basin tribes include the **Shoshone** tribe, the **Ute** tribe, and the **Washo** tribe.

Apache Wickiup

SOUTHWEST REGION

The dry southwest was home to Native Americans who built their dwellings from adobe bricks. The **Apache** tribe, the **Pueblo** tribe, and the **Navajo Nation** all lived in different sections of this region.

Elderly 99 year old Navajo Native American woman and her daughter standing in front of a traditional Hogan.

GREAT PLAINS REGION

The huge expanse of the Great Plains was suitable for nomadic tribes. These groups of Native Americans hunted the bison for food so they set up their teepees, hunted the herds, and then traveled to the new locations when the herds moved. The tribes there were made famous in Westerns. They are the **Blackfoot,** the **Comanche,** the **Crow,** the **Cheyenne,** and the **Arapahoe** tribes.

Teepee in American prairie near Grand Canyon
Skywalk build by Hulapai tribe

Iroquois Longhouse

NORTHEAST WOODLANDS REGION

This region had a powerful league of Native Americans connected by the Iroquois language. In addition to the **Iroquois League,** the **Wappani** tribe as well as the **Shawnee** tribe lived here.

Seminole Indian Tribe Hut

SOUTHEAST REGION

One of the largest tribes, the Cherokee, lived in this region. In Florida, the *Seminole* tribe lived in the Everglades. The *Chickasaw* people lived in what is now the Mississippi and Alabama regions. These tribes sustained themselves through farming.

MAJOR GROUPS OF NATIVE AMERICANS BY LANGUAGE

Another way for historians to study the Native American groups is by the languages or cultures they shared.

ALGONQUIAN

Over 100 different tribes spoke languages that are described as Algonquian. These tribes eventually spread across the entire continental United States and included the *Blackfoot tribe*, the *Cheyenne tribe*, the *Mohican tribe*, and the *Ottawas*.

Blackfoot warrior, (Karl Bodmer, between 1840 and 1843)

APACHE

At least six different tribes spoke the language of *Apache*.

View of a Native American Apache camp, Arizona, shows a Chiricahua Apache medicine man with his family inside a brush wickiup.

Seneca Cayuga Onondaga Oneida Mohawk Tuscarora

IROQUOIS

The five Native American tribes that were part of the *Iroquois League* were the *Seneca tribe*, the *Onondaga tribe*, the *Mohawk tribe*, the *Oneida tribe*, and the *Cayuga tribe*. The *Tuscarora people* also joined their alliance later on. These nations were all closely located in the northeastern part of the United States.

3 Iroquois Warriors with weapons.

SIOUX

The Sioux Nation was organized into three large groups including the Lakota tribe, the Western Dakota tribe, and the Eastern Dakota tribe.

Native American Sioux chief Sitting Bull, (c. 1831-1890).

THE LARGEST NATIVE AMERICAN TRIBES TODAY

Many Native Americans were forced to relocate and leave their native regions. After the Indian Removal Act in 1830, about 125,000 Native Americans occupied lands in the states of Georgia, Tennessee, and Alabama as well as North Carolina and Florida. White settlers wanted to grow cotton on these lands, so the United States government made the Native Americans leave their homelands. They were forced to walk for a journey of thousands

Colorful Native American Regalia at a Summer Pow Wow.

of miles to live in a new **"Indian territory"** that had been designated for them. This journey is called the **"Trail of Tears"** because many died along the way.

The last census data in the United States ranks these ten tribes as those with the most population. About 22% of all Native Americans still live on reservations that were dictated by the United States government during the Indian Removal Act.

NAVAJO - 308,000 members

CHEROKEE - 285,000 members

SIOUX – 131,000 members

CHIPPEWA – 115,000 members

CHOCTAW – 88,000 members

APACHE – 64,000 members

PUEBLO – 59,000 members

IROQUOIS – 48,000 members

CREEK – 44,000 members

BLACKFOOT – 23,000 members

Native American dancer.

The San Manuel Band of Indians hold their annual Pow Wow in San Bernardino.

Now you know more about the 10 largest Native American tribes and some of the important history of Native Americans before and after the Europeans arrived. You can find more American History books from Baby Professor by searching the website of your favorite book retailer.

Visit

BABY PROFESSOR
EDUCATION KIDS

www.BabyProfessorBooks.com

to download Free Baby Professor eBooks
and view our catalog of new and exciting
Children's Books

CPSIA information can be obtained
at www.ICGtesting.com
Printed in the USA
BVHW010749011020
590075BV00012B/192